MW01254667

BITTER OR BETTER

A PERSONAL WALK THROUGH GRIEF

Keith & Debbie

I was saddened to
learn of your mother's death.
Please know of my concern &
prayer support for your family.
I know that memories become
precious with time.

Don

BITTER OR BETTER
A PERSONAL WALK THROUGH GRIEF

DON FORRESTER

TATE PUBLISHING
AND ENTERPRISES, LLC

Published by Tate Publishing & Enterprises, LLC
127 E. Trade Center Terrace | Mustang, Oklahoma 73064 USA
1.888.361.9473 | www.tatepublishing.com

Tate Publishing is committed to excellence in the publishing industry. The company reflects the philosophy established by the founders, based on Psalm 68:11,
"The Lord gave the word and great was the company of those who published it."

Book design copyright © 2015 by Tate Publishing, LLC. All rights reserved.
Cover design by Ivan Charlem Igot
Interior design by Jomel Pepito

Published in the United States of America

ISBN: 978-1-63449-109-9
1. Biography & Autobiography / Personal Memoirs
2. Self-Help / Death, Grief, Bereavement
14.11.27

This book is dedicated posthumously to the men and women who served in Vietnam and didn't return and to their families whose lives were forever changed.

CONTENTS

PREFACE

I am not an expert on the grief process, but I do know that it is not quickly nor easily resolved. I have never encountered the loss of a mate or that of a child. In terms of familial relationships, I cannot begin to imagine the range of emotions or the overriding sense of sadness that must accompany such a loss. I have, however, experienced loss up close and personal. It is out of that experience that I share the following reflections.

LOSS: UP CLOSE AND PERSONAL

I'll never forget the day that Treva and I happily made our way to Odessa for the wedding of her brother. It was Friday, December 29, 1972. We arrived in town early and stopped for a brief visit with my folks prior to going to the home of her family.

We were met at the door by a long-term family friend who ushered us into my parent's home. I could tell from the look on her face that something was terribly wrong. It was then that we were confronted with the news that two marines had just left my parent's home after informing them that my brother's aircraft was missing somewhere over North Vietnam. My brother was now classified as missing in action.

Reportedly, the A-6 Intruder aircraft in which he was flying had left the military base in Nam Phong, Thailand two days earlier for a night mission over North Vietnam. When the aircraft failed to return to the base at the anticipated hour, efforts were made to locate the downed aircraft, but to no avail.

The marines who had delivered the news reminded my parents of our responsibility as a family to maintain hope. Reportedly, the United States Marine Corps would do everything possible to locate and safely return my brother. It was now up to us, his family, to maintain hope. We owed it to our loved one.

THE GRIEF PROCESS

What a roller coaster of emotions! How does one inundated with an overwhelming sense of sadness also maintain hope for a safe return? Balancing the two extremes became one of the greatest challenges I've ever faced.

On a feeling level, initially I felt half dead. It was unmistakable. As a twin, my brother and I shared a special bond. He had always been there. He was a part of my identity. People referred to us as twins. We were regarded as a unit. It was as though half of who I am had disappeared. The sense of loss was debilitating. It was closely akin to someone knocking the breath out of you. You gasp for air and find it difficult to breathe. You know you have to breathe, but breathing represents one painful difficulty after another.

Across four decades, I still remember the uncontrollable anguished crying that I permitted myself in the privacy of the bath as I showered later that evening. (I say I permitted it. Actually, I've never had that kind of control.) The flood of tears came involuntarily. Never have I experienced such anguish and agony.

The tears that flowed out of a sense of intense pain that evening have resurfaced on many occasions since that time. Perhaps at every crossroad or developmental level, I am reminded of my brother's loss and the missed blessings of his companionship and camaraderie. What I've learned through the process is that tears are healthy. They express that which cannot be expressed in any other forum. Even as I write the words, I find myself teary eyed and grateful with remembrance.

Subsequently, across four decades, I have discovered what a treasured gift memory becomes. Somehow, with the passing of time, memories become more precious and less painful. Memory serves as a catalyst prompting a spirit of gratitude and thanksgiving for times shared. How wonderful it is to remember the joy of my brother's presence and the gift of love that memory supplies.

Initially, memory was not nearly as palatable. Memory served only as a painful reminder of loss and the brutality of war. It became a temporary quagmire that threatened to debilitate with an overriding sense of pain.

In the weeks and months that followed, I was oftentimes blindsided emotionally as I processed the dimensions of grief. I'd turn a corner and see a car like the one he drove and break into tears. I'd hear a song on the radio that we both used to listen to, and tears would stream down my cheeks. I'd run across a mutual childhood friend and become teary eyed. Everywhere I turned, there were vivid reminders of his presence. Each reminder underscored the pain associated with his loss. Initially, it seemed like one very long continuum.

Eventually, with the passing of time, the conscious awareness of grief begins not to darken the totality of every day. The pursuit of living brings with it opportunities and challenges that offer diversion and respite from some of the sense of loss. Life places family, friends, opportunities, work responsibilities, and a variety of other good things to assist in offering a diversion that precludes life from becoming one dimensional and totally absorbed in perpetual sadness. The dawning of a new day emotionally does not come quickly, but it does eventually offer an upside to the dreadful reminders of loss.

Despite the invitation of other pursuits, reminders from the past can often catch one unaware.

- I was at a meeting in a hotel conference room on Congress Avenue in Austin a couple of years following my brother's status as MIA. The Aggie Band and Corps of Cadets came marching down Congress Avenue in parade fashion. The last time I had seen the corps in parade fashion was at final review during my brother's senior year at A&M. It was an emotional moment; I was deluged with a flood of tears.

- The first time I flew as a passenger in a private airplane following the loss of my brother and absorbed the visual dimensions of the earth from an altitude where vision seemed unlimited, I was instinctively reminded of him. Flying was the love of his life. Even though I was not flying the plane, seeing the earth from that perspective brought a flood of memories and the tears clouded my vision.

- I did not attend my ten-year high school reunion. Consequently, when the twenty-year reunion rolled around, it was something I wanted to attend. For whatever reason, following graduation from high school, I lost contact with the majority of friends from my earlier years. The twenty-year reunion offered an opportunity to renew acquaintances. It was something I wanted to do. I attended the reunion and as anticipated enjoyed the opportunity immensely. The following day, as I made the six-hour trip back home, the pain of my brother's absence was the catalyst for an overwhelming sense of renewed grief. I literally cried all the way home.

- Managing an empty chair at the holidays is not an easy process. Perhaps because my brother's plane went down during the Christmas bombing raids over North Vietnam, the holiday season often triggers a subtle reminder of his loss.

- Several years ago, I went to see the movie *For the Boys* with Bette Midler. It was an overview of the life experience of a USO singer reflecting back over three wartime experiences. It caught me unawares. I went home and cried for hours.

- At the wedding of my niece (who was only two years of age when her father's plane went down), she asked me privately before the wedding began, "Would you like to see what I'm wearing that is old?" She lifted up the hem of her wedding dress. Sewed to the inside edge was the name badge from one of her father's military uniforms. She had sewn it on the side where her dad should have been standing. My eyes filled with tears as we shared a tender moment.

My sense is that one is never totally free from the grief process. When one loves intensely, that love is never ending. Consequently, how that love subsequently manifests itself becomes the challenge.

WHERE DOES ANGER FIT IN?

I am not a person who lives with an ongoing sense of anger. There have been few times in my life when anger was an emotion with which I've had to deal. Yet I cannot chronicle the grief experience related to my brother's loss without referencing the emotion of anger. It was an issue that merited resolution.

I was only twenty-five years old when I lost my brother. He was only twenty-five. We were both negotiating the demands of young adulthood—marriage and family, parenting, careers, opportunities, spiritual growth, etc. The list goes on and on. Nowhere on the list of what we anticipated life would bring was the need to manage without the other. It was never a consideration. Consequently, the reality of his absence seemed so terribly brutal and unfair. I was not prepared for the loss. Someone had to be responsible for this injustice!

Anger toward the President. Initially, President Nixon was an easy target for my anger. After all, it was he who ordered the Christmas bombing raids of 1972. Reportedly, the president made the decision to bomb Hanoi with a "best guess" of the causality count that would result. From my personal perspective, the stakes were way too high, and whatever "outcome measures" were used to calculate the mission were radically miscalculated.

Shortly before my brother's plane went down, he was flying a mission over North Vietnam in a squadron of other military aircraft. During that mission, he observed the plane of two of his best friends exploding in the air. The plane apparently had been hit by a surface-to-air missile. There was no way that either of the two men on board escaped. Predictably, it was a very upsetting experience for him. He wrote home that nothing they were doing was "worth the lives" of those two men.

Part of the problem was the continued fixed flight pattern that pilots were required to fly. Despite the fact that the Vietnamese had a fairly elaborate system of surface-to-air missiles, squadrons out of Thailand were ordered to fly the same route day after day. Military personnel planning the missions discounted the threat of the fixed surface-to-air missiles already in place. There was no variety in the route pilots were ordered to fly.

It was easy to conclude that the military had to own some of the responsibility for the awful sense of injustice I was experiencing. Our president made the decision to bomb Hanoi knowing full well the projected casualty count. From my perspective, the price of admission was way too high.

Anger toward God. Part of the anger I subsequently experienced was directed toward God. After all, didn't He have the resourcefulness to preclude a tragedy of this magnitude? What about the prayers I had spoken concerning my brother's welfare and safety? Never was there a day that I didn't ask for God's watch and care over my brother. Did my prayers fall on deaf ears? Where was God when my brother's plane went down?

God, out of His gracious Spirit, allowed me to ask question after question. Somewhere in the process, it occurred to me that I wasn't big enough to take God on. What nerve on my part! It was almost the same reminder that Job had been given. God reminded me that all that I had experienced that contributed meaning and purpose to life was not a result of my own doing. It was all a gift beyond my deserving. God was still God, and He had the ability and wherewithal to manage all that I was experiencing. Somehow, I emerged from that experience with a renewed confidence in God's ability to provide.

About twenty years later, I was reminded of that brief encounter with God by observing the relationship and interaction between my son and daughter. My son followed in his uncle's footsteps and graduated from Texas A&M. Upon graduation, he was commissioned as an officer in the US Marine Corps.

Despite the ten-year-age difference, my daughter has always been supportive of her brother. While he was in basic training at Quantico, Virginia, she wrote to him frequently. One day, she inadvertently laid a letter she had written to him on the coffee table in our home. I normally don't read mail intended for another, but after the second or third day, I picked it up and quickly scanned the well wishes she was sending his way. At the bottom, she had written a postscript, "Craig, I pray for you every day. I ask God to keep you safe."

I put the letter down as tears filled my eyes. I couldn't help but wonder what it would do to her childlike faith if something happened to her brother? I very protectively wanted to shield her from that. As an adult, I knew from experience that without faith in God there ultimately is nothing that offers meaning and purpose to life. My daughter was potentially too young and fragile to have that same sense of reference. I did not want her faith to be tested.

Across the years, I have encountered a number of people who do not attest to have a faith relationship with God. They unapologetically describe themselves as agnostic. They don't have a faith in God that offers resilience and support. From their observation and experience, the presence of God and the reality of His unconditional love through the gift of redemption and His day-to-day support are simply nonexistent.

I have had the opportunity to get to know some of these folks personally. Almost without fail, in all of their pasts, each encountered circumstances where they became painfully aware of their need for God's intervention and support. It may have been a life-threatening accident or illness of a mate, a parent or a child. Each pleaded with God to do something. In seemingly childlike faith, they pleaded for the healing and restoration of their loved one. At face value, their prayers went unanswered. The disappointment and heartache that resulted became the basis for their intuitively discounting the reality of a loving God who desires relationship and supports our greatest good.

How grateful I am that God did not allow my spirit to struggle in this regard.

Anger toward Myself. I quickly moved from being angry with God to being angry with myself. Although, at age twenty-five, we all have a tendency to consider ourselves immortal, I felt I should have known better. I should have done something. I was intelligent enough to know the risks associated with being a bombardier navigator in the military. Why didn't I do something to intervene in my brother's behalf? Surely I could have said something, done something, intervened in some way that would have resulted in a different outcome. Surely I could have persuaded him not to volunteer early for a tour of duty that placed him in harm's way. The squadron he was assigned to in North Carolina never saw active duty in Vietnam. The war ended before his group would have been called to serve.

I guess hindsight is always 20/20. Unfortunately life does not have a rewind button. We can't go back and erase the past. Our only option is to negotiate life in the present and look forward to the future. I missed an opportunity to make an impact that might have orchestrated a different outcome. I simply didn't know.

Anger toward My Brother. Surprisingly, for a brief period of time I was extremely angry with my brother. It was his loss that had plummeted me into the abyss of despair. Never had I experienced such pain. To emerge from that experience angry with him seemed incomprehensible. Yet it was difficult not to conclude that the career options my brother chose ultimately placed his entire family in harm's way. What was he thinking? If he didn't have the presence of mind to consider risks to himself, how selfish he must have been to ignore what became our ultimate plight.

Where does anger fit in? Based on my own experience, I'd have to say that anger is probably a temptation that accompanies every grief experience. Unfortunately, it carries with it the potential to debilitate and destroy.

I am fortunate to have experienced the negative impact associated with anger for only a brief encounter.

Across the years, as both a social worker and pastor, I have periodically come in contact with people whose lives seem to be motivated by anger. They present themselves as even tempered. They are always mad. Their lives represent that which seems void of joy, peace, a sense of calm, and a hope for the future. For them the glass is always half empty, never full. Perhaps allowed to go unchecked, anger manifests itself in this dimension. The ultimate outcome is always one of emptiness and despair.

This should not come as a surprise. The New Testament overview of God is one of unconditional love and forgiveness. We see a God who is always ready to reclaim and renew. The parables of the lost sheep, the lost coin, and the prodigal son all highlight God's desire to recover the brokenness of our humanity through the grace that is available under the watchfulness of His care.

Life brings with it the opportunity for us to allow Him to role-model His forgiveness through us. Truthfully, I had to come to the place where I could offer wholesale forgiveness related to the loss of my brother.

AN ABILITY TO WALK
AND FAINT NOT

I mentioned earlier the challenge of balancing the overwhelming sense of sadness associated with the loss of my brother and that of maintaining hope for his safe return.

Part of the expectations initially shared with our family and subsequently reinforced at every briefing over several years by representatives of the United States Marine Corps, was the need for us to do our part in maintaining hope for my brother's eventual safe return. It was a clear mandate. We owed it to our loved one.

We were reminded that the military would continue their ongoing reconnaissance effort and that we could best serve our loved one by continuing with life as before while we put our best foot forward in anticipation of his eventual return. At their suggestion, there were some things we could do.

- We were to refrain from any newspaper coverage related to my brother's circumstances and his status as MIA. We were told that North Vietnam had the resources to solicit any news-release information, even in a place as remote as the *Odessa American*, and would undoubtedly use it to negatively impact my brother.

- It would obviously be a betrayal of our loved one to hold any kind of commemoration or public expression of grief related to his circumstances. After all, we were only negotiating a time-limited loss. My brother would be safely returned to us.
- We could allow the military to do their job. We had to trust that they had the resources and expertise to expeditiously right this wrong that had been thrust on our family. It was just a matter of time. My brother would be located and safely returned.

On a feeling level, the aforementioned suggestions were a tough assignment. How did one continue to negotiate life without incurring any negative impact or sense of loss associated with what seemed like imminent peril?

Perhaps on a feeling level, it was easier to follow the military mandate to maintain hope for my brother's eventual safe return than to be confronted with the overwhelming sense of loss we would have experienced as a family had we had proof of his death.

Through the years, as a pastor, I have had the opportunity to share with families through some of life's darkest hours.

I have repeatedly observed the value of families and friends coming together to consolidate and unify their understanding of grief through a time of commemoration and tribute to the memory of loved ones. From what I've been able to observe, coupled with my own experience of subsequent losses through death in my extended family, the public consolidated effort of a funeral serves as a helpful tool to strengthen families and reinforce support and eventual hope for ultimate family reunification in eternity.

At a time when such an experience would have held value and been meaningful, it was not an option we could employ. We were pretty well relegated to managing our grief related to our loss in isolation. There was not a forum for any kind of extended family or collective friendship support to sort out feelings related to the death of my brother. We were all relegated to maintaining hopes and prayers for his eventual safe return.

That is not to say that extended family and close family friends did not provide comfort and go the second and third mile in being attentive to our needs. We were the recipients of wonderful support, love and caring. It is simply that in managing our loss, the focus was always on our ability to maintain hope as we anticipated my brother's safe return. We did not address the issue of his permanent loss this side of eternity.

Our family was fortunate to have a faith relationship with the Lord. He ministered to each of us in our times of need. We experienced the promises of His word when He said, "Come to me, all you who are weary and burdened and I will give you rest" (Matthew 11:28, niv). He was for us a balm in Gilead.

In the back of each of our minds was the inevitable question, what if my brother did not return? We were comforted by the knowledge that Ron too had a personal walk with the Lord. I had talked with him just prior to his departure for Thailand. He was confident in his relationship with the Lord. The what-if issue was not a problem. If my brother perished in Vietnam, we had the certainty that in death he would be with the Lord. That hope provided great comfort. It's just that we were not yet as a family to the place where we could deal with that eventuality without feeling somehow we were betraying and abandoning my brother.

The military had made it clear that our job was to maintain hope for my brother's eventual return. Perhaps even without that mandate, we would have been resistive to the notion that Ron wasn't coming back. Without any evidence to support his death, it was logical we'd maintain some semblance of hope. It was a difficult dilemma.

The Lord literally provided the resources to assist us in negotiating the day-to-day demands of living. Experience was a painful teacher that the loss we were experiencing was not one that would be expeditiously resolved. The days turned into weeks, the weeks into months, and the months became perpetual.

In reflecting back over that extremely sad time in my life, I can clearly remember the circumstances surrounding the eventual homecoming of those who had been held prisoners of war by Vietnam. The night when Vietnam released the names of prisoners who were to be returned to the United States was a slow one. It was somewhere after 2:00 a.m. that our contact with the military telephoned to confirm that my brother's name was not on the list.

The bitter news was like a second assault to my already fragile spirit. We had maintained such hope! How could his name not appear on the list of those prisoners that Vietnam was returning home? It was inconceivable.

No sooner had the list of prisoners scheduled for return to the United States been released than a multiple of unanswered questions surfaced. There were hundreds of men previously identified as MIA who were known to be POW. Their names were not included on the lists of prisoners being returned. They were names for whom Vietnam gave no accounting. What had happened to those men?

The injustice of it all and the silence surrounding the unanswered questions was cause for grave concern. It was clear to many that the North Vietnamese were not playing by the rules. They had failed to provide a full accounting for men previously known to be POW. They had not fulfilled their agreement negotiating the end of the war.

The League of Families, an organization comprised of family members and interested others and whose primary purpose was to advocate for the safe return of all missing servicemen, was incensed at the lack of thoroughness with which North Vietnam only gave lip service to their agreement to provide a full accounting.

Again the message was clear. It was articulated by the League of Families. It was reinforced by contacts with the military. We were to maintain hope. We had to rely on our government to handle the crisis, press for a full accounting, and somehow resolve the discrepancy between the number of prisoners returned from the war and the number our military intelligence knew for certain were known POW.

The subsequent televised return of American POWs returning from Vietnam was an emotional experience. Many US servicemen would emerge from the airplane that brought them back to the United States and intuitively kneel to kiss the ground out of gratitude to finally be back on American soil. The faces of family members and those of former POWs were teary eyed yet radiant with joy. I too watched those proceedings teary eyed. I was grateful for the safe return and joyful reunions of so many. At the same time, there was an intense longing in my heart to know the same joy other families were experiencing. The pain was intense.

In the weeks that followed, I paid close attention to the limited information coming out of Washington related to the plight of Americans relegated to the limbo of being classified as MIA. There was appropriate rhetoric demanding a full accounting for all men classified as MIA and those who were known to be POW who were not returned. North Vietnam adamantly maintained they had done their part in meeting the terms of the Paris Peace Accords. It was an impasse.

Despite rhetoric pressing Vietnam for more details and demanding a full accounting, my impression of the primary attitude coming out of Washington was a "let's cut our losses mentality" and move on. Americans wanted to distance themselves from any remembrance of a war we did not win.

Later, under the leadership of the League of Families, in an effort to appeal for some kind of humanitarian response by the government of North Vietnam, a "We Think It's Important" campaign was initiated, calling on Americans to mail a tablespoon of American soil to leaders of Vietnam. It was felt that because of the Vietnamese reverence for homeland, this ploy might make an impact in their perception of the need to exercise civility in rendering a full accounting. I don't know how successful the campaign proved to be in terms of American participation, but the ploy was ineffectual in making a dent toward a more detailed accounting on the part of North Vietnam.

One of the things that did work in soliciting American awareness regarding the plight of the POW/MIA issue was the POW/MIA bracelets. Their origin began the decade before my brother was listed as MIA. The metal bracelets were imprinted with the name, rank, and date of the serviceman's POW/MIA status. It was the intent that the person wearing the bracelet would do so until the serviceman was returned. The bracelet was intended to look like a handcuff. I personally never wore one. My life was already inundated with reminders of loss everywhere I turned. The thought of wearing a bracelet to further exaggerate that awareness was more than I could handle. Yet whenever I saw anyone wearing a POW/MIA bracelet regardless of the name inscribed, I experienced a feeling of gratitude. I always felt appreciative and indebted to folks who did what they could to promote an awareness of the issues and advocate for some kind of resolution.

Despite periodic wide circulation of rumors regarding live sightings of Americans being held in Vietnam, there was always a lack of official confirmation to substantiate the reports. Posturing of the general public related to the possibility of Americans still held in Vietnam or transferred to prison camps in Russia, Siberia, or elsewhere was always one of disbelief. As shared earlier, part of the expectations initially shared with our family and subsequently reinforced at every briefing over a several-years period by representatives of the Marine Corps was the need for us to do our part in maintaining hope for my brother's eventual safe return. It was a clear mandate. We owed it to our loved one. Perhaps, from an emotional standpoint, that posture was also the least intrusive for it allowed us to maintain some semblance of hope that one day our family would be reunited.

Almost with no warning, the rules changed and the expectations shifted. Six years following my brother's status as MIA, administrative decisions were made by order of the president for a unilateral shift in category of all servicemen listed as MIA. Their status was to be changed from MIA to killed in action/body not recovered (KIA/BNR).

It was an emotional assault! How, after six years of encouragement to maintain hope, were we to dispel those hopes and prayers and shift to a posture of hopelessness? The rules changed. In order for us to successfully appeal the presidential mandate for change of status, it then became incumbent on the family to offer proof to substantiate our loved one was alive.

At the time, it almost seemed like the proverbial straw that broke the camel's back. From an emotional standpoint, how were we to manage? We were encouraged by the military to formalize our grief experience. They offered the services of a military chaplain if we desired a memorial service or any kind of symbolic internment for my brother. My brother had said prior to his deployment to Thailand that if anything happened to him, he'd like to be buried at Arlington National Cemetery. There was an area in the cemetery for placement of a headstone in an area dedicated as a memorial hill. A decision was made to honor his request and participate in a military funeral and symbolic burial through placement of a headstone.

Six year earlier, the value of such a service might have been more meaningful. After six years of attempting to repress any thought that my brother might not return, it was difficult to accept the paradigm shift without any supporting evidence to substantiate his death. Perhaps that has something to do with human nature.

A memorial service fifteen hundred miles from the place my brother called home, six years following his loss, almost seemed anticlimactic. At best, it seemed surreal. I don't remember much about the service. We were so few in number that the almost empty sanctuary seemed institutional and cold. We had not met the chaplain prior to the service. Consequently, when he rose to speak, it was as if we were being addressed by a stranger. Perhaps it was the best that could be expected. Truthfully, the chaplain and other military personnel with whom we had interaction that day presented themselves as empathetic and kind.

About ten years after the loss of my brother, I received a telephone call from my former sister-in-law, who had remarried. She began the conversation with, "Sit down, I've got some news for you…" Over the next several minutes, she chronicled for me a series of events—recent contacts initiated by military personnel with whom there had been years of silence, former friends of my brother who were still in the Marine Corps who "passed through town" and stopped to visit. It was her conclusion based on a renewal of many events that the government had reason to believe my brother was alive.

What hopeful news! The explanation for all the contacts subsequently proved to be one of coincidence and happenstance. However, for a brief interval, my spirit was lightened with the energy I gleaned from that solitary telephone call offering a ray of hope. Interestingly, as Easter rolled around the following month, I encountered the good news of the resurrection with far more feeling than I'd ever experienced before. For the first time in my life, based on recent experience, I had a frame of reference to begin to understand from the disciples' perspective how it had to feel to make the discovery of Christ's resurrection.

I have heard that delayed gratification is a sign of maturity. Perhaps somewhere along the way, I came of age. From an emotional and spiritual perspective, God has given me a peace that the message of Easter provides all of the assurances and hope I need to manage the demands of the day.

ALL THINGS
WORK TOGETHER FOR GOOD

For the last thirty plus years, I have had the privilege of serving as pastor to a group of the most caring and supportive people I've ever known. Truthfully, their prayer support, continual affirmation of His Word, gentle redirection when needed, and words of encouragement and support have been a Godsend. Through the leadership of His Spirit, God has provided everything needed to enrich and support my life.

The value of sharing life with a family of faith that is supportive, caring, and focused on His Word and unconditional love has been instrumental in orchestrating an overall sense of well-being in my life. Had I not experienced loss up close and personal, I would not have a frame of reference to know how empty and dark the night of grief can be. I also know firsthand and personally the emergence of hope that comes from the resiliency of His Spirit from within.

Please don't mistake what I'm saying. God did not cause my brother's plane to go down in order to teach me a lesson or two about living. There are two forces at work in the world. The tempter is the one whose intent it is to destroy and disrupt all that God intended. He is the author of war, not God. But what I am saying is God allowed me to ultimately benefit from the experience.

The awareness of His support and care across the years has strengthened my faith. Though I am far from a perfect pastor, I can truthfully say that I never counsel with a family in the midst of life's darkest hour without knowing intuitively what that experience feels like for the family member. Fortunately, I also have a frame of reference to know the outcome of His sustaining grace.

The surreal experience of attending the memorial ceremony for my brother and having a total stranger conduct the service always serves as a subtle reminder to do things differently. I am always honored to be invited to share with a family in life's time of trials. Consequently, I respond to that privilege with an obligation to know the family before the funeral. Even when I have been asked to conduct a service for someone whom I do not know, I always make an opportunity to visit with the family and find out about their loved one prior to the funeral. Across the years, I have met a lot of people posthumously through visits with family and friends that I would have enjoyed knowing personally. I always benefit from the experience.

I guess, like a lot of other people, I'd have to admit that what limited spiritual growth I have experienced has been wrought from the vantage point of giving up on myself and allowing Him to be the strength in my life. Though far from spiritually mature, I have to admit that in looking back over those things that have most shaped my faith, much of it has been an outgrowth of His sustaining grace when I did not have the resources in and of myself to rise to the challenge.

Several months ago, I had an opportunity to attend the funeral for the mother of a long-term friend. It is not often that I have occasion to sit in the pew and view a funeral service from the vantage point of someone in attendance rather than shouldering responsibility for sharing a word of comfort and hope. As I listened to the pastor share a personal word about his relationship with my friend's mother and her dad, the thought occurred to me that I have been blessed beyond measure to have been given so many opportunities across the years to share with families through some of life's darkest hours.

I have been permitted to share in the circle of emotions and the expressions of inner thoughts shared by family members as they have confronted the sad reality of their separation from loved ones. These experiences are such a contrast to the casual, surface-relationship dialogue that far too often summarizes our conversations with others—times when we discuss the weather, sports, automobiles, politics, etc.

When confronted with life and death issues, folks generally are far more open in sharing inner thoughts and feelings. It is almost as if the barriers we establish to distance ourselves from others collapse in the midst of crisis and people risk sharing that which matters most. That process in the midst of Christian compassion cements relationships and bonds families and friends together.

Later, in reflecting on the funeral service, I realized anew how fortunate I have been to have had the privilege of ministering in the same community for over three decades. I have been blessed to be in a church family where folks have regarded me as family. They have freely and openly allowed me to share in the intimacy of that which matters most.

The role of pastor has placed me in a strategic position to share with others as they are called to negotiate things in life that truly matter. Through the process, there has been a mutual exchange of information. In the process of helping, I have been helped. In the process of caring, I have been the recipient of care. In the process of loving, I have experienced the joy of being loved. My life has been filled with the abundance of shared relationships provided in part due to the nature of a role, that of pastor. That which matters most to me has been given by others.

For those who continue to struggle with the grief process, please hear me say that I know the difficulty and challenge that represents. Based on my limited experience, I am not sure that one ever actually brings the process totally to closure. Even four decades later, tangible reminders of loss can quicken a memory and revive an emotion.

Three or four years before my dad's death, I attended a family update session in Dallas with representatives from the various branches of armed services to discuss recovery efforts for the US military personnel declared MIA in previous wars. It had been years since I last participated in a League of Families meeting or a military-sponsored family update.

I arrived an hour early for the family update meeting and was startled by the size of the meeting room and the large number of chairs available for family members who had preregistered to attend. Watching the participants arrive, I was curious about the age ranges and family compositions attending the meeting. While there were a number of participants in their early thirties, the vast majority of those attending were significantly older.

One of the more interesting aspects of the meeting was an introduction of each family represented and a subsequent time for questions and answers. As several family members related their last contact with loved ones or last known information concerning their status, I was surprised at the range of emotions that surfaced as family members discussed their loved ones.

One lady shared that she received a letter from her brother in May 1952. Subsequently, the family received notification a few days later of his capture in Korea. Two years later, they were notified that her brother died in captivity. Her voice broke as she expressed her commitment to advocate for the return of his body to US soil. Her story repeated itself a dozen times over as family members from the Korean Conflict expressed hopes of the eventual return of the remains of their loved ones.

It became clear to me by observing those present that the grief process is not quickly nor easily resolved. Some of the family members in attendance have carried the agony of not knowing the details of their loved one's fate for almost five decades.

From the level of emotion shared, it seemed to me that many of the older individuals present, who are now nearing the final chapter of their own lives, are intent on bringing closure to the open wounds of unfinished business related to disposition of the remains of missing family members. Families protectively and perhaps memorably want to ensure a final resting place in the United States.

As I read between the lines of the worn and tired faces of my parents, who also are negotiating the final chapter of their earthly existence, their hope is not dissimilar from that expressed by others in the room. If remains can be recovered, they want them brought home.

I left the meeting convinced that war is hell on earth and that its devastation passes on from one generation to the next. All across the room, there were painful reminders on the facial expressions of those present that lack of closure continues to disturb and create pain.

Later reflection helped me to focus on the sufficiency of His grace to negotiate the painful circumstances of war. Apart from the hope we have in Christ, I can think of nothing else that can make a lasting difference. For the child of God, death is not final; it is only a time of separation. For those of us whose families have been forever changed due to the ravages of war, we have the promise of Christ when he said, "I will be with you always, even until the end of the world" (Matthew 28:20, niv).

UNEXPECTED GIFTS

Several months after the war ended, our family received a letter from one of Ron's friends in the military. Dennie Mounts had been stationed at the same Marine Corps base in North Carolina. Their paths subsequently met again in Thailand.

Dennie shared the details of his last conversation with my brother. My brother was very saddened by the recent loss of two mutual friends who were Marine Corps pilots that he and Dennie both knew. Ron had witnessed the explosion of their aircraft as it was brought down by a surface-to-air missile. According to Dennie, his conversation with my brother centered around that loss, along with a discussion regarding the things in life that ultimately matter. My brother was certain of his relationship with the Lord and the assurances he held concerning his fate for all eternity.

Ron maintained great hope for the future. He was ready for the war to end and looked forward to the opportunity of returning home. There was so much about life that he treasured. He was eager to reexperience that which had been left behind and forfeited for the war effort. According to Dennie, Ron made the affirmation that he had much to live for, but if that was not to be, he would live with God through all eternity. Ron had a peace concerning his fate.

The gift of Dennie's unsolicited letter was an act of Christian kindness. It was clear from the correspondence that he was managing his own grief related to the loss of my brother and that of other friends lost in the war. He too shared the Christian faith and affirmed what a treasured gift my brother's friendship had meant to him personally.

My brother's best friend was a friend from our childhood. When we were growing up, David Moss lived three houses down on our block. David's life also represented the epitome of the Christian faith. He treasured the relationship he shared with my brother. When David's first child was born, David and Janie named him after my brother in honor of Ron's memory. What a special gift of kindness!

(Reflecting back on the debt of gratitude I carry for Dennie and David has left me teary eyed. Shortly after the war ended, Dennie and his wife returned to his family's farm in Oklahoma. We received notification a short time after receiving Dennie's letter that he had been killed in a farming accident. David Moss went on to become district attorney in Tulsa, Oklahoma. At the age of forty-eight, he suffered a heart attack and died at his home.)

The gift of springtime always reminds me of God's gift to mankind through the Easter event. Perhaps it is for that reason that Easter is my favorite holiday. Unlike other holidays, such as Thanksgiving or Christmas, where it is easy to notice an empty chair at the table due to the absence or loss of a loved one, it is almost as though Easter is dedicated to their memory. Easter serves as a reminder that we will one day be reunited with those who have gone on to be with the Lord.

The apostle Paul wrote to the church at Thessalonica:

> Brothers and sisters, we do not want you to be uninformed about those who sleep in death , so that you do not grieve like the rest of mankind, who have no hope. For we believe that Jesus died and rose again, and so we believe that God will bring with Jesus those that have fallen asleep in him. (1 Thessalonians 4:13–14) niv]

I read somewhere that Winston Churchill, the English statesman and man of courage who did much to orchestrate a victory for the allies in World War II, planned his own funeral. Churchill selected St Paul's Cathedral in London as the site for his funeral. As the service was concluding, according to Churchill's instructions, a bugler positioned somewhere in the dome of the great Cathedral played the song "Taps" to signal the end of day. No sooner had the bugler concluded than another musician located elsewhere in the dome began playing the notes of "Reveille": "It's time to get up. It's time to get up. It's time to get up in the morning."

Churchill was right. Because of Easter, the last note will not be "Taps" but "Reveille." As trees, shrubs, and grass begin to shed the dead of winter and come alive with new growth and freshness, nature always reminds me of the promises of God for those who place their faith in Him.

The gift of memory has become such a treasured tool. It is fun to reminisce, particularly with family and friends, of the wonderful times shared from childhood and in our young adult years. Growing up as a twin is a special gift. It also has a downside. Until we revolted, my mother ensured that we were always dressed alike. Consequently, if there was a button missing from a shirt, Ron generally was able to determine it had to belong to me. I like to think I held my own. We were friends. We shared a special bond. I am grateful for the experience. Memory makes it all possible to reflect on time and time again. For that I am grateful.

About ten years ago, my younger brother Larry made me aware that he had discovered, quite by accident, that there is a website designed in memory of Ron. A friend had suggested he type his own name into a search engine and see what came up. There was no match. Out of curiosity, he typed in Ronald W. Forrester and discovered a volume of information.

Stacy Jones, a young woman who lives in Texarkana, designed a website as a school project. She became interested in the MIA issue and wanted to do something to preserve the memory of some of the men who lost their lives in Vietnam. Robert Routh, one of my brother's friends from high school discovered the website and communicated via email with Stacy. Subsequently, he forwarded his own reflections related to the gift of my brother's friendship, and she added those reflections to the website.

We initiated communication with Stacy who expressed an eagerness to know more about my brother. At my suggestion, Larry sent some information he had written and Stacy established another link to the website to chronicle that information.

The creativity and gift of a stranger to pay tribute to my brother and preserve his memory is something for which I will always be grateful. I guess at some level all of us would like to think our lives are invested in that which matters. Stacy has effectively communicated that Ron's contributions did make a difference.

One of the most meaningful and unexpected gifts came through the referral from a couple who occasionally worship in our church. They asked if I'd visit with one of their friends who was having a tough time. Their friend had been abruptly thrust into the precipitously painful process of managing the sense of loss and grief resulting from the untimely deaths of his twin brother and his niece and two nephews. Their lives had been forfeited by the careless and unconscionable actions of an intoxicated truck driver.

From the moment I met Eric Groten, our spirits connected, and I have been greatly blessed by the gift of his friendship. I don't have the words to describe the bond we intuitively shared other than divine appointment. Our friendship is one that does not require a lot of contact to remain vital, significant, and valued. In many respects we have little in common. He is significantly younger, extremely bright, a respected and skilled attorney, and actively involved in a hundred and one things that demand his attention. We live in very different worlds, but his friendship is one that lends value and worth to my being.

About a year after I met him, my friend incurred another overwhelming personal tragedy. His two children were killed in a plane crash along with their mother and her husband. Somehow through it all, my friend has found the resourcefulness of God to "walk and faint not" (Isaiah 40:31). He credits the success and periodic struggles and pitfalls of that painful journey to the proven dependability of God's love. He intuitively and perceptively knows that it will always be a work in progress.

Several months later, I received a telephone voicemail from my friend, who called to notify me of the birth of his son. His message left me with tears streaming down my face. His son's birth date was on the anniversary of his children's death. Even now, as I share his voice message, it quickens my spirit. "We are feeling very well indeed—mind, body, and soul."

My friend's life is a miracle. He has confronted issues and circumstances that would immobilize others. I have heard it said that people emerge from tragedy with one of two outcomes. They either become better or they become bitter. Perhaps the key to my friend's success and his humble spirit is his acknowledgement that somehow God has provided.

EPILOGUE

Two decades ago, my brother's daughter, a college student at Texas A&M received a large envelope of materials from the US Marine Corps. There was no cover letter with the included materials. The envelope simply contained a lengthy document described as a crash-site investigation report. The report contained detailed testimony solicited from villagers in a province in North Vietnam concerning their recollection of a plane crash thought to be associated with my brother. The document contained fairly gruesome details related to decapitation and dismemberment of body parts of one of the pilots who was recovered. Reportedly, a leg was subsequently buried in a villager's hog pen. There was no explanation provided concerning disposition of the rest of the remains. It was reported that the other pilot perished in the plane.

The report contained fairly diverse testimony related to the time the crash took place. Testimony was as diverse as a ten-year period. In addition, some small pieces of aircraft reportedly were recovered. The recovered pieces did not match the type of aircraft in which my brother was flying.

Trust me, after years of silence and waiting, no one is more interested in knowing the details and circumstances of my brother's fate than his family. We welcome whatever information we can obtain. The investigative report my niece received contained so many discrepancies, including reference to airplane parts that were not a match to the plane he flew, that we questioned the credibility of the conclusion.

We responded to the report in writing. We thanked the military for the information and affirmed our willingness and desire to receive any information pertinent to my brother. However, we did highlight the contradictory information and asked on what basis they reached the conclusion that the reported crash site was his. Their written response indicated they had made a mistake. In looking more carefully at the information, they too concluded that the crash site could not have been that of my brother's.

That report was followed by six more years of silence. Reportedly, at that time, another crash-site investigation team revisited the same province and concluded the crash site had to be that of my brother. This time, the investigatory team located the downed aircraft in a canal. However, it could not be accessed because the aircraft was submerged in approximately ten feet of quickly moving water. In addition, the canal contained poisonous snakes. We subsequently learned that the investigating team was reportedly scheduled to complete a crash-site excavation of what was thought to be my brother's plane in May or June 2002. Those months were chosen because they reflected the dry weather season in that province of North Vietnam. When we subsequently asked for a report, we were told that no excavation had been scheduled and that no team had gone back into the area.

Perhaps we will never know for certain.

In looking back over the four decades since the loss of my brother, I can truthfully say that at no point have I been a stranger to God's grace. Across the last four decades, I have experienced and reexperienced every possible range of emotion. Through it all, I've never experienced it in isolation. God has always been there. He has been the support system that energized my spirit, comforted my pain, and offered hope for the beginning of a new dawn. He has provided the ability to walk and not faint.

I cannot pinpoint a timeline when I experienced a shift in that for which I hoped and prayed. In the initial weeks, months, and years following the loss of my brother, I longed for his return. That longing was never far from my conscious awareness. Somewhere along the way, however, it became a greater comfort to think of him with the Lord than his continuing to struggle for survival in a land where he was separated from his family and friends.

It is a simple fact—war does not have a positive face. It seeks to debilitate and destroy. It forever disrupts a family unit and forever alters what might have been. It destroys hopes and dreams for the here and now, but it ultimately cannot win. Because of Christ, there is no death, only a time of transition.

Ronnie and Donnie

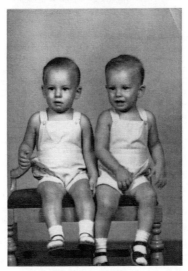

Ronnie and Donnie

Ronnie and Donnie

Ronnie - Senior Year - Texas A&M

Ronnie - Texas A&M

Back row - Ronnie, Donnie, Larry
Front row - Wayne and Neva

Don Forrester

Neva, Wayne, Ronnie, Larry, and Donnie

Ronnie and Donnie

Larry, Wayne, Ronnie, Donnie, Bill

Ronnie and Donnie

Jana & Ronnie - Wedding

Larry, Donnie, Ronnie

Jana, Ronnie, Karoni